ROOTED

ISBN 13: 978-1-4621-2347-6

Published by CFI, an imprint of Cedar Fort, Inc.
2373 W. 700 S., Springville, UT 84663
Distributed by Cedar Fort, Inc., www.cedarfort.com

Cover design by Shawnda T. Craig

Layout by Shawnda T. Craig
Edited by Kathryn Watkins and Nicole Terry

Printed in the United States of America

10 9 8 7 6 5 4 3 2

Printed on acid-free paper

Al Carraway

ROOTED

Scripture Study Journal

CFI • An imprint of Cedar Fort, Inc. • Springville, Utah

Other products by Al Carraway

More than the Tattooed Mormon

Cheers to Eternity!

Wildly Optimistic

You've Got This! (contributor)

With God Life Is Oh So Good—journal

Set Goals. Say Prayers. Work Hard—journal

I Know—journal

FOREWORD

If you follow me on any social platform you know that as a result of joining The Church of Jesus Christ of Latter-day Saints, I lost everyone. I faced disapproval and fighting and silence from my family. Longtime friends wanted nothing to do with me, and *oh* how it hurt to see how easily and quickly they left. There were several times that my coworkers and my boss would bring me into their offices and make me watch all of these terrible and untrue videos about the gospel. They would tell me that I was a terrible person and what I had become a part of was wrong. How hard that was just being baptized and feeling like I was being punished for doing what I thought was the right thing. I didn't know what to do or how to defend myself because I had only known of the Church for only a few weeks at that time. How small my knowledge was.

In early membership, so many things just fell apart. I'd never known loneliness *until* I got baptized. I'd never known such painful sacrifice and loss *until* I joined the Church. I'd never known real pain until then. Indescribable anguish. I'd never struggled so long and so hard where my body would literally ache, until I got baptized.

Having never been brought up in the language of scriptures, the Book of Mormon made *no* sense to me. But I read it, at first only because I told the missionaries I would. I read it at first because they promised me great things and I was set to prove them wrong. But after gaining a testimony and with the great loss that followed baptism, I desperately read, looking for the promised blessings because it's all I had to hold on to. Most times it felt as though all I had was God and His Word. But in all times, that is the power we need.

In my ignorance and awkwardness and desperation, I pleaded and searched and guessed and experimented to figure it out. Picking it up every free second I had, revived and pumped life and power into my soul. Do you know how many hard decisions and unexpected steps I've taken because of ideas I had while reading?! I'm desperately grateful for its capacity to reel me back to what I need to be focusing on and working toward. To be very literal, I'm not sure what I'd do without that book. It's how my hope has been able to stay intact.

It's where comfort and confidence have come, where perspective and promise have been rebuilt. As a result of having the Book of Mormon between my soul and God, I have developed a deep-rooted love and reliance on that book. Because of it all, I *know* God. And I love Him with a real love. And I wouldn't trade that knowledge and relationship for anything.

Simply put, I am not without it. I am not strong. I am not confident. I am not wise or smart. I am not guided. I get it. I was a stubborn, independent 21-year-old New Yorker who thought she could conquer the world on her own. But if it weren't for giving scripture a *real* chance daily, even when it didn't make sense to me at first and even though I didn't really want to, I wouldn't be here. I wouldn't have what I have. I would not truly be happy. I would not truly be me without it—*without Him*. And I hope that everyone will give this book a real effort and allow themselves to be changed and blessed the way I have been.

The secret to losing weight? Work. The secret to good grades? Work. The secret to getting a strong testimony? Work. The secret to keeping your testimony strong? Work. But how can we think the gospel isn't for us if we aren't actively learning about it and living it? If we aren't working at it? How can He answer us when we do not speak to Him? How can we expect answers and change and progress and growth if we aren't actively searching, asking, and listening every day?

We have to continuously choose Him over the fleeting things of this world. We have to stay focused. We have to give God the time He deserves. We have to make taking care of us *and our soul* a priority—make God a priority. Because this isn't wishful thinking—*it's real*. All of it. And nothing is worth giving up our forever happiness.

And if you haven't yet, give Him the chance to show you how great your God truly is. Actively live the way you should to give Him the opportunity to show you the better way. Comfort, strength, energy, and hope are always there for you, because God and His resources are right here in front of you. It all lies within the simple things of the gospel that are too often overlooked.

Because the reality is you have a real soul living within you, and it's crucial to feed it. Can you think of anything more important than endless happiness and eternal life?! Let's give this a real go at it! Every day. Because *wow*, what an indescribable difference I don't dare live without again. Because nothing is worth giving up that comes from God. Because time and time again, through unwanted, unexpected, and uncharted paths, God has brought me to the better things.

The other morning when I got home from the gym, I saw my husband at our dining room table, and he was just . . . sitting there. And it looked like he was maybe crying? I couldn't tell. So, I sat down and asked what was up, and he said, "He did it again." The week before, Ben had felt that he really needed to turn his scripture study into an active and intentional "feast" every day for that week, holding weight and surety that he knew something specific (but unknown) was going to come from it.

And because he did that, he and I actually received some pretty big counsel that week that left us sitting at our table together for two hours talking about everything he thought of and felt, as unexpected revelation and correction brought us in a new direction that just blossomed and unfolded as we discussed it together. Confusion and conflict about some decision-making became a new and exciting path with determination and surety.

Someone recently asked me what I thought the impact of the Book of Mormon was, and I never answered them. But I think that right there is part of the impact. If we invest and if we are intentional, if we listen to subtle thoughts that come when we're seeking, if we pay attention to reoccurring ideas, if we take time to explore and talk spiritually with our family—we'll have these moments where we just . . . sit there. And with tears in our eyes we'll think, *He did it again*. And then we'll move forward with determination through our unexpected correction and exciting change of course as we let life blossom from allowing ourselves to let God be God in our lives.

“We need to feel, deep in ‘the inmost part’ of our hearts, that the Book of Mormon *is* unequivocally the word of God. We must feel it so deeply that we would never want to live even one day without it.”

—President Nelson

“Viewpoint” *Church News* October 29, 2017

GETTING STARTED

[**ROOTED—adj.:** to be rooted in the scriptures, rooted in your testimony, rooted in the gospel, and deeply rooted in your relationship with your Savior.]

The word of God is the scriptures, and within the scriptures is a power to feed and pump life to the soul living within us. If we allow that power into our lives, our very souls will be impressed upon and changed by the Holy Ghost and our understanding of our Savior will increase. It's a powerful source to heal hurting hearts and wounded souls and for receiving revelation to life's questions and trials to keep us moving forward, onward and upward. Within those hallowed pages there is power to strengthen, comfort, change, encourage, counsel, warn, resist, teach, answer, revive, convert, solve, bless, protect, and so much more. "Scriptures are like packets of light that illuminate our minds and give place to guidance and inspiration from on high" (Richard G. Scott, "The Power of Scriptures," *Ensign*, November 2011).

But to unlock the power, in order to take root and grow like a seed, it requires consistent, daily effort, actively searching, praying, listening, and seeking. I hope that through these study prompts, your love for the scriptures will blossom and you will become deeply rooted in our Savior.

WHAT'S INSIDE

Within these pages, you will find a first of its kind study prompt journal designed to increase scripture understanding and personal revelation. Filled with space for notes, favorite verses, goals, testimony, answered prayers, and a 365-day reading chart, my hope is that you will use these tools in the ways that work for you personally. Consider these pages the rich soil you can use to grow your testimony seed.

STUDY TIPS

START WITH PRAYER—Be honest with the Lord in what you're thinking, feeling, and wondering about. Specific prayers receive specific answers. God speaks to us through the Holy Ghost. Ask to clearly understand His promptings.

KEEP PERSPECTIVE—Try to see things the way the Lord sees things. Trust that God's ways are higher than our ways and that God's timing is measured different than our timing. Answers may not always come immediately, but strength and comfort and guidance always will, and with consistent effort comes growth and understanding.

CHANGE—What we learn should lead us to change. Act on promptings. Use the goals section in this journal to keep track of progress and impressions.

PAUSE—Take time to sit in silence and listen to your thoughts and feelings. Pay attention to your good, reoccurring thoughts, That's usually how the spirit subtly speaks to me. Pay especially close attention to thoughts that seem irrelevant to what you're reading. Remember all good things come from God, including any feelings of comfort, hope, strength, forgiveness, happiness, perspective, etc. It's how He communicates to us and shows He is there for us, even if answers aren't.

END WITH PRAYER—Thank God for insights, promptings, and feelings you may have received. Commit and ask for help to live what you learned. Continue to have honest and open conversation. Sometimes it helps to picture God standing right in front of us, to speak to Him as if speaking face to face.

TIPS FOR MAKING MORE TIME FOR SCRIPTURES

I definitely know it's not about how fast we get through the scriptures. But knowing the strength and revelation that comes from reading them, I know it *is* about how *often* we read them so we can receive even more help from them.

EASY THINGS TO DO

1. **READ EVERY DAY.** Set a specific time to read that will work for you daily and make it a habit. Lunchtime, before school/work—even if it means setting your alarm a little earlier. I prefer to read as soon as I wake up, when the world is quiet but the spirit is not—breakfast for me and breakfast for my soul.

2. **DON'T WAIT FOR QUIET.** I've been humbled & surprised every time I read during chaotic playtime around my kids. *Almost* every time they see me read, they grab a book and start "reading" too. Or when I get caught up in silly things and I see Ben reading at the table, I adjust my priorities. The impact of doing it around others is much greater than us. A girl told me that her mom has never read the Book of Mormon, and that made her sad and confused. Then she found out when she was older that her mom read it daily but she was always alone during nap time or bedtime.

3. **DON'T LIMIT HOW MUCH TO READ.** Instead of saying I'll read X amount of verses a day and stop, just read until you can't read anymore for whatever reason.

4. **IT'S OK TO READ MORE THAN ONCE A DAY.** What?! I know. And it will make a huge contrast in yourself and your life when you do this. And do you know how much you can gain if you watch just one less episode on Netflix? Or how much you can get from a few verses while you're waiting for your water to boil? Or waiting in the car for your friend/kid to come out?

5. **KEEP A BOOK OF MORMON *EVERYWHERE*.** I know the convenience and blessings of the Gospel Library app, which is great, but I'm talkin' hard copies so you can see it and be reminded of it in times when you wouldn't be otherwise. Keep one in your bathroom, on your kitchen counter, and at your bedside. Pocket-sized ones are perfect for your car and purse. (*You can get them for free from the missionaries, or if you live in high populated member areas, D.I. and thrift stores have some awesome ones for a quarter.*)

6. **START OVER.** When you finish, celebrate and be excited! Soak it in. Gloat a little even to yourself for accomplishing it. But then turn it right back to page one and start from the beginning. A week, or a month, or the start of next year are not appropriate lengths for parties.

FAVORITE VERSES

GOALS

- Short Term -

Goal: ______________________________
____
____

☐ Goal reached! Date goal made: __________ Date to reach goal: __________

Goal: ______________________________
____
____

☐ Goal reached! Date goal made: __________ Date to reach goal: __________

Goal: ______________________________
____
____

☐ Goal reached! Date goal made: __________ Date to reach goal: __________

Goal: ______________________________
____
____

☐ Goal reached! Date goal made: __________ Date to reach goal: __________

GOALS

- Long Term -

Goal: ____

____

____

☐ Goal reached! Date goal made: __________ Date to reach goal: __________

Goal: ____

____

____

☐ Goal reached! Date goal made: __________ Date to reach goal: __________

Goal: ____

____

____

☐ Goal reached! Date goal made: __________ Date to reach goal: __________

Goal: ____

____

____

☐ Goal reached! Date goal made: __________ Date to reach goal: __________

GOALS

- Short Term -

Goal: ____________________

☐ Goal reached! Date goal made: __________ Date to reach goal: __________

Goal: ____________________

☐ Goal reached! Date goal made: __________ Date to reach goal: __________

Goal: ____________________

☐ Goal reached! Date goal made: __________ Date to reach goal: __________

Goal: ____________________

☐ Goal reached! Date goal made: __________ Date to reach goal: __________

GOALS

- Long Term -

Goal: ____________________

____

____

☐ Goal reached! Date goal made: __________ Date to reach goal: __________

Goal: ____________________

____

____

☐ Goal reached! Date goal made: __________ Date to reach goal: __________

Goal: ____________________

____

____

☐ Goal reached! Date goal made: __________ Date to reach goal: __________

Goal: ____________________

____

____

☐ Goal reached! Date goal made: __________ Date to reach goal: __________

GOALS

- Short Term -

Goal: ____________________

____

____

☐ Goal reached! Date goal made: __________ Date to reach goal: __________

Goal: ____________________

____

____

☐ Goal reached! Date goal made: __________ Date to reach goal: __________

Goal: ____________________

____

____

☐ Goal reached! Date goal made: __________ Date to reach goal: __________

Goal: ____________________

____

____

☐ Goal reached! Date goal made: __________ Date to reach goal: __________

GOALS

- Long Term -

Goal: ____

____

____

☐ Goal reached! Date goal made: __________ Date to reach goal: __________

Goal: ____

____

____

☐ Goal reached! Date goal made: __________ Date to reach goal: __________

Goal: ____

____

____

☐ Goal reached! Date goal made: __________ Date to reach goal: __________

Goal: ____

____

____

☐ Goal reached! Date goal made: __________ Date to reach goal: __________

ANSWERED PRAYERS

/ / :

/ / :

/ / :

/ / :

/ / :

/ / :

/ / :

/ / :

/ / :

/ / :

/ / :

/ / :

/ / :

/ / :

/ / :

DATE: 10/21

WHERE I READ:

Alma 14

What's happening: Believers are burned - Alma & Amulek are ridiculed but are the only ones to survive prison collapse.

What doctrine is being taught? Faith in Christ & submitting to His will. Plan of salvation & judgment v.11

A talk or scripture that relates to this: Abinadi was also not willing to deny his faith in Christ & suffered death by fire - Mosiah 17

Favorite verse from today's reading: "Perhaps they will burn us also - be it according to the will of the Lord." v.12&13

INSPIRING WORDS OR VERSES:

1. According to their faith
2. The Lord granted unto them power
3. Everyone was slain except A&A - protection & huge miracle

THEMES I SAW:

1. Accepting God's will - Keeping the faith
2.
3.

Recurring thoughts (impressions, feelings, revelations) especially the ones unrelated to what I'm reading:

Confidence comes from accepting God's will fully. Our faith is not in vain, even if hard times don't let up right away. Would A&A love & know God as well if God made it so prison never happened & they never experienced its destruction & their incredible protection?

What did I think and feel as I read? Comfort in His guidance. More confident to let things unfold as is knowing God is in charge.

What Christlike attribute(s) did I notice? Humility, Alma had faith in saving others-but submitted to the Lord's will when that was not what God wanted in those situations. Integrity from believers who sacrificed their life & from A&A when they were persecuted & abused. Faith in Christ knowing He is our Savior, which lead to conviction from both believers & A&A.

REPETITIVE PHRASES THAT STUCK OUT TO ME:

1. 'power of God'
2.
3.

→

How have I seen this in my life? It's our unwanted & our hard that allow us to know & understand God better than ever! When A&A were in prison, sometimes I question why I am in certain situations & why He allowed me to get there but once I see it through, I see His hand & receive better blessings.

How can I follow the example of this person from the scriptures?

Be able to look at my trials or change of courses with a "so be it" outlook like Alma in v.13, knowing who is guiding me. Be content with God's will.

How does what I read today apply to me? Or my day today?

I think we can relate to a sense of despair & hopelessness to not be able to save or protect those around us that are suffering v.10

Putting our desires or expectations before God's. Blaming God or wonder where He is in our hard or unwanted. Standing firm in beliefs & values during modern day persecution.

What does this teach me about Christ?

He is all knowing & all loving. He honors our faith & sacrifices.

Regardless of passing time, He will show us He never left us & His power comes through IF we stay close to Him

What am I doing well?

Honest, conversational prayers.

Looking for another perspective outside my limited desires & vision.

What questions do I have? what good can come from things not going how I planned? what's God's current will for me?

How did today's reading change my perspective? Are we going to complain that we are "captive" or struggling, or are we going to hold out faithful for a bigger miracle? (v.28) v.10 when they wanted to save those burning but the spirit "constraineth me" helped me understand the eternal purposes of God better - all things are done in the wisdom of God.

What does God want me to know right now? Trust Him more vastly. Your faith will not avoid trials but it will protect you & lead you to bigger miracles. You will make it

TODAY I AM GRATEFUL FOR:

Added perspective for God & my trials.

What can I change or work on?

Remembering there's great peace & confidence that comes from fully accepting God being with us through everything, especially the bad & the hard.

DATE: ____________

WHERE I READ:

____

What's happening: ______________________________

____

____

____

What doctrine is being taught? ______________________________

____

____

A talk or scripture that relates to this: ______________________________

____

____

Favorite verse from today's reading: ______________________________

____

____

INSPIRING WORDS OR VERSES:

1. ______________________________
2. ______________________________
3. ______________________________

THEMES I SAW:

1. ______

2. ______

3. ______

Recurring thoughts (impressions, feelings, revelations) especially the ones unrelated to what I'm reading:

What did I think and feel as I read?

What Christlike attribute(s) did I notice?

REPETITIVE PHRASES THAT STUCK OUT TO ME:

1. ______

2. ______

3. ______

→

How have I seen this in my life?

How can I follow the example of this person from the scriptures?

How does what I read today apply to me? Or my day today?

What does this teach me about Christ?

What am I doing well?

What questions do I have?

How did today's reading change my perspective?

What does God want me to know right now?

TODAY I AM GRATEFUL FOR:

What can I change or work on?

DATE: ______________

WHERE I READ:

____

What's happening: ______________________________________
____
____
____

What doctrine is being taught? ____________________________
____
____

A talk or scripture that relates to this: _____________________
____
____

Favorite verse from today's reading: ________________________
____
____

INSPIRING WORDS OR VERSES:

1. ______________________________
2. ______________________________
3. ______________________________

THEMES I SAW:

1. ______________________________
2. ______________________________
3. ______________________________

Recurring thoughts (impressions, feelings, revelations) especially the ones unrelated to what I'm reading:

What did I think and feel as I read?

What Christlike attribute(s) did I notice?

REPETITIVE PHRASES THAT STUCK OUT TO ME:

1. ______________________________
2. ______________________________
3. ______________________________

How have I seen this in my life? ______

How can I follow the example of this person from the scriptures?

How does what I read today apply to me? Or my day today?

What does this teach me about Christ?

What am I doing well?

What questions do I have?

How did today's reading change my perspective?

What does God want me to know right now?

TODAY I AM GRATEFUL FOR:

What can I change or work on?

DATE: ______________

WHERE I READ:

____

What's happening: ___________________________________

____

____

____

What doctrine is being taught? ___________________________________

____

____

A talk or scripture that relates to this: ___________________________________

____

____

Favorite verse from today's reading: ___________________________________

____

____

INSPIRING WORDS OR VERSES:

1. ___________________________________
2. ___________________________________
3. ___________________________________

THEMES I SAW:

1. ____________________

2. ____________________

3. ____________________

Recurring thoughts (impressions, feelings, revelations) especially the ones unrelated to what I'm reading:

What did I think and feel as I read?

What Christlike attribute(s) did I notice?

REPETITIVE PHRASES THAT STUCK OUT TO ME:

1. ____________________

2. ____________________

3. ____________________

How have I seen this in my life?

How can I follow the example of this person from the scriptures?

How does what I read today apply to me? Or my day today?

What does this teach me about Christ?

What am I doing well?

What questions do I have?

How did today's reading change my perspective?

What does God want me to know right now?

TODAY I AM GRATEFUL FOR:

What can I change or work on?

DATE: ______________

WHERE I READ:

____

What's happening: ___________________________________
____
____
____

What doctrine is being taught? ___________________________________
____
____

A talk or scripture that relates to this: ___________________________________
____
____

Favorite verse from today's reading: ___________________________________
____
____

INSPIRING WORDS OR VERSES:

1. ___________________________________
2. ___________________________________
3. ___________________________________

THEMES I SAW:

1. ______________________________

2. ______________________________

3. ______________________________

Recurring thoughts (impressions, feelings, revelations) especially the ones unrelated to what I'm reading:

What did I think and feel as I read?

What Christlike attribute(s) did I notice?

REPETITIVE PHRASES THAT STUCK OUT TO ME:

1. ______________________________

2. ______________________________

3. ______________________________

How have I seen this in my life?

How can I follow the example of this person from the scriptures?

How does what I read today apply to me? Or my day today?

What does this teach me about Christ?

What am I doing well?

What questions do I have?

How did today's reading change my perspective?

What does God want me to know right now?

TODAY I AM GRATEFUL FOR:

What can I change or work on?

DATE: ____________

WHERE I READ:

____

What's happening: ______________________________

What doctrine is being taught? ______________________________

A talk or scripture that relates to this: ______________________________

Favorite verse from today's reading: ______________________________

INSPIRING WORDS OR VERSES:

1. ______________________________
2. ______________________________
3. ______________________________

THEMES I SAW:

1.
2.
3.

Recurring thoughts (impressions, feelings, revelations) especially the ones unrelated to what I'm reading:

What did I think and feel as I read?

What Christlike attribute(s) did I notice?

REPETITIVE PHRASES THAT STUCK OUT TO ME:

1.
2.
3.

How have I seen this in my life?

How can I follow the example of this person from the scriptures?

How does what I read today apply to me? Or my day today?

What does this teach me about Christ?

What am I doing well?

What questions do I have?

How did today's reading change my perspective?

What does God want me to know right now?

TODAY I AM GRATEFUL FOR:

What can I change or work on?

DATE: ______________

WHERE I READ:

____

What's happening: ____

____

____

____

What doctrine is being taught? ____

____

____

A talk or scripture that relates to this: ____

____

____

Favorite verse from today's reading: ____

____

____

INSPIRING WORDS OR VERSES:

1. ____
2. ____
3. ____

THEMES I SAW:

1. ______________________________

2. ______________________________

3. ______________________________

Recurring thoughts (impressions, feelings, revelations) especially the ones unrelated to what I'm reading:

What did I think and feel as I read?

What Christlike attribute(s) did I notice?

REPETITIVE PHRASES THAT STUCK OUT TO ME:

1. ______________________________

2. ______________________________

3. ______________________________

How have I seen this in my life?

How can I follow the example of this person from the scriptures?

How does what I read today apply to me? Or my day today?

What does this teach me about Christ?

What am I doing well?

What questions do I have?

How did today's reading change my perspective?

What does God want me to know right now?

TODAY I AM GRATEFUL FOR:

What can I change or work on?

DATE: ______________

WHERE I READ:

____

What's happening: ____

What doctrine is being taught? __________________________________

A talk or scripture that relates to this: ___________________________

Favorite verse from today's reading: ______________________________

INSPIRING WORDS OR VERSES:

1. ____
2. ____
3. ____

THEMES I SAW:

1. ______________________________
2. ______________________________
3. ______________________________

Recurring thoughts (impressions, feelings, revelations) especially the ones unrelated to what I'm reading:

What did I think and feel as I read?

What Christlike attribute(s) did I notice?

REPETITIVE PHRASES THAT STUCK OUT TO ME:

1. ______________________________
2. ______________________________
3. ______________________________

How have I seen this in my life?

How can I follow the example of this person from the scriptures?

How does what I read today apply to me? Or my day today?

What does this teach me about Christ?

What am I doing well?

What questions do I have?

How did today's reading change my perspective?

What does God want me to know right now?

TODAY I AM GRATEFUL FOR:

What can I change or work on?

DATE: ____________

WHERE I READ:

____

What's happening: ______________________________

____

____

____

What doctrine is being taught? ______________________________

____

____

A talk or scripture that relates to this: ______________________________

____

____

Favorite verse from today's reading: ______________________________

____

____

INSPIRING WORDS OR VERSES:

1. ______________________________
2. ______________________________
3. ______________________________

THEMES I SAW:

1. ______________________________

2. ______________________________

3. ______________________________

Recurring thoughts (impressions, feelings, revelations) especially the ones unrelated to what I'm reading:

What did I think and feel as I read?

What Christlike attribute(s) did I notice?

REPETITIVE PHRASES THAT STUCK OUT TO ME:

1. ______________________________

2. ______________________________

3. ______________________________

→

How have I seen this in my life?

How can I follow the example of this person from the scriptures?

How does what I read today apply to me? Or my day today?

What does this teach me about Christ?

What am I doing well?

What questions do I have?

How did today's reading change my perspective?

What does God want me to know right now?

TODAY I AM GRATEFUL FOR:

What can I change or work on?

DATE: ______________

WHERE I READ:

____

What's happening: ___________________________________

____

____

____

What doctrine is being taught? ___________________________________

____

____

A talk or scripture that relates to this: ___________________________________

____

____

Favorite verse from today's reading: ___________________________________

____

____

INSPIRING WORDS OR VERSES:

1. ___________________________________
2. ___________________________________
3. ___________________________________

THEMES I SAW:

1. ______

2. ______

3. ______

Recurring thoughts (impressions, feelings, revelations) especially the ones unrelated to what I'm reading:

What did I think and feel as I read?

What Christlike attribute(s) did I notice?

REPETITIVE PHRASES THAT STUCK OUT TO ME:

1. ______

2. ______

3. ______

→

How have I seen this in my life?

How can I follow the example of this person from the scriptures?

How does what I read today apply to me? Or my day today?

What does this teach me about Christ?

What am I doing well?

What questions do I have?

How did today's reading change my perspective?

What does God want me to know right now?

TODAY I AM GRATEFUL FOR:

What can I change or work on?

DATE: ______________

WHERE I READ:

____

What's happening: ______________________________

____

____

____

What doctrine is being taught? ______________________________

____

____

A talk or scripture that relates to this: ______________________________

____

____

Favorite verse from today's reading: ______________________________

____

____

INSPIRING WORDS OR VERSES:

1. ______________________________
2. ______________________________
3. ______________________________

THEMES I SAW:

1. ______________________________
2. ______________________________
3. ______________________________

Recurring thoughts (impressions, feelings, revelations) especially the ones unrelated to what I'm reading:

What did I think and feel as I read?

What Christlike attribute(s) did I notice?

REPETITIVE PHRASES THAT STUCK OUT TO ME:

1. ______________________________
2. ______________________________
3. ______________________________

How have I seen this in my life?

How can I follow the example of this person from the scriptures?

How does what I read today apply to me? Or my day today?

What does this teach me about Christ?

What am I doing well?

What questions do I have?

How did today's reading change my perspective?

What does God want me to know right now?

TODAY I AM GRATEFUL FOR:

What can I change or work on?

DATE: ______________

WHERE I READ:

____

What's happening: ____________________________________

____

____

____

What doctrine is being taught? ____________________________________

____

____

A talk or scripture that relates to this: ____________________________________

____

____

Favorite verse from today's reading: ____________________________________

____

____

INSPIRING WORDS OR VERSES:

1. ____________________________________
2. ____________________________________
3. ____________________________________

THEMES I SAW:

1. ________________

2. ________________

3. ________________

Recurring thoughts (impressions, feelings, revelations) especially the ones unrelated to what I'm reading:

What did I think and feel as I read?

What Christlike attribute(s) did I notice?

REPETITIVE PHRASES THAT STUCK OUT TO ME:

1. ________________

2. ________________

3. ________________

How have I seen this in my life?

How can I follow the example of this person from the scriptures?

How does what I read today apply to me? Or my day today?

What does this teach me about Christ?

What am I doing well?

What questions do I have?

How did today's reading change my perspective?

What does God want me to know right now?

TODAY I AM GRATEFUL FOR:

What can I change or work on?

DATE: ____________

WHERE I READ:

____

What's happening: ________________________________

____

____

____

What doctrine is being taught? ________________________________

____

____

A talk or scripture that relates to this: ________________________________

____

____

Favorite verse from today's reading: ________________________________

____

____

INSPIRING WORDS OR VERSES:

1. ________________________________
2. ________________________________
3. ________________________________

THEMES I SAW:

1. ______________________________

2. ______________________________

3. ______________________________

Recurring thoughts (impressions, feelings, revelations) especially the ones unrelated to what I'm reading:

What did I think and feel as I read?

What Christlike attribute(s) did I notice?

REPETITIVE PHRASES THAT STUCK OUT TO ME:

1. ______________________________

2. ______________________________

3. ______________________________

How have I seen this in my life?

How can I follow the example of this person from the scriptures?

How does what I read today apply to me? Or my day today?

What does this teach me about Christ?

What am I doing well?

What questions do I have?

How did today's reading change my perspective?

What does God want me to know right now?

TODAY I AM GRATEFUL FOR:

What can I change or work on?

DATE: ______________

WHERE I READ:

____

What's happening: ___________________________________

____

____

____

What doctrine is being taught? ___________________________________

____

____

A talk or scripture that relates to this: ___________________________________

____

____

Favorite verse from today's reading: ___________________________________

____

____

INSPIRING WORDS OR VERSES:

1. ___________________________________
2. ___________________________________
3. ___________________________________

THEMES I SAW:

1. ______________________________

2. ______________________________

3. ______________________________

Recurring thoughts (impressions, feelings, revelations) especially the ones unrelated to what I'm reading:

What did I think and feel as I read?

What Christlike attribute(s) did I notice?

REPETITIVE PHRASES THAT STUCK OUT TO ME:

1. ______________________________

2. ______________________________

3. ______________________________

→

How have I seen this in my life? ______

How can I follow the example of this person from the scriptures?

How does what I read today apply to me? Or my day today?

What does this teach me about Christ?

What am I doing well?

What questions do I have?

How did today's reading change my perspective?

What does God want me to know right now?

TODAY I AM GRATEFUL FOR:

What can I change or work on?

DATE: ______________

WHERE I READ:

____

What's happening: ______________________________

____

____

____

What doctrine is being taught? ______________________________

____

____

A talk or scripture that relates to this: ______________________________

____

____

Favorite verse from today's reading: ______________________________

____

____

INSPIRING WORDS OR VERSES:

1. ______________________________
2. ______________________________
3. ______________________________

THEMES I SAW:

1. ______________________________

2. ______________________________

3. ______________________________

Recurring thoughts (impressions, feelings, revelations) especially the ones unrelated to what I'm reading:

What did I think and feel as I read?

What Christlike attribute(s) did I notice?

REPETITIVE PHRASES THAT STUCK OUT TO ME:

1. ______________________________

2. ______________________________

3. ______________________________

→

How have I seen this in my life?

How can I follow the example of this person from the scriptures?

How does what I read today apply to me? Or my day today?

What does this teach me about Christ?

What am I doing well?

What questions do I have?

How did today's reading change my perspective?

What does God want me to know right now?

TODAY I AM GRATEFUL FOR:

What can I change or work on?

DATE: ____________

WHERE I READ:

____

What's happening: ______________________________

____

____

____

What doctrine is being taught? ______________________________

____

____

A talk or scripture that relates to this: ______________________________

____

____

Favorite verse from today's reading: ______________________________

____

____

INSPIRING WORDS OR VERSES:

1. ______________________________
2. ______________________________
3. ______________________________

THEMES I SAW:

1. ______________________________

2. ______________________________

3. ______________________________

Recurring thoughts (impressions, feelings, revelations) especially the ones unrelated to what I'm reading:

What did I think and feel as I read?

What Christlike attribute(s) did I notice?

REPETITIVE PHRASES THAT STUCK OUT TO ME:

1. ______________________________

2. ______________________________

3. ______________________________

How have I seen this in my life?

How can I follow the example of this person from the scriptures?

How does what I read today apply to me? Or my day today?

What does this teach me about Christ?

What am I doing well?

What questions do I have?

How did today's reading change my perspective?

What does God want me to know right now?

TODAY I AM GRATEFUL FOR:

What can I change or work on?

DATE: ______________

WHERE I READ:

____

What's happening: ______________________________

____

____

____

What doctrine is being taught? ______________________________

____

____

A talk or scripture that relates to this: ______________________________

____

____

Favorite verse from today's reading: ______________________________

____

____

INSPIRING WORDS OR VERSES:

1. ______________________________
2. ______________________________
3. ______________________________

THEMES I SAW:

1. ___

2. ___

3. ___

Recurring thoughts (impressions, feelings, revelations) especially the ones unrelated to what I'm reading:

What did I think and feel as I read?

What Christlike attribute(s) did I notice?

REPETITIVE PHRASES THAT STUCK OUT TO ME:

1. ___

2. ___

3. ___

How have I seen this in my life?

How can I follow the example of this person from the scriptures?

How does what I read today apply to me? Or my day today?

What does this teach me about Christ?

What am I doing well?

What questions do I have?

How did today's reading change my perspective?

What does God want me to know right now?

TODAY I AM GRATEFUL FOR:

What can I change or work on?

DATE: ____________

WHERE I READ:

____

What's happening: ______________________________

____

____

____

What doctrine is being taught? ______________________________

____

____

A talk or scripture that relates to this: ______________________________

____

____

Favorite verse from today's reading: ______________________________

____

____

INSPIRING WORDS OR VERSES:

1. ______________________________
2. ______________________________
3. ______________________________

THEMES I SAW:

1. ______________________________

2. ______________________________

3. ______________________________

Recurring thoughts (impressions, feelings, revelations) especially the ones unrelated to what I'm reading:

What did I think and feel as I read?

What Christlike attribute(s) did I notice?

REPETITIVE PHRASES THAT STUCK OUT TO ME:

1. ______________________________

2. ______________________________

3. ______________________________

How have I seen this in my life?

How can I follow the example of this person from the scriptures?

How does what I read today apply to me? Or my day today?

What does this teach me about Christ?

What am I doing well?

What questions do I have?

How did today's reading change my perspective?

What does God want me to know right now?

TODAY I AM GRATEFUL FOR:

What can I change or work on?

DATE: ______________

WHERE I READ:

____

What's happening: ____

____

____

____

What doctrine is being taught? ____

____

____

A talk or scripture that relates to this: ____

____

____

Favorite verse from today's reading: ____

____

____

INSPIRING WORDS OR VERSES:

1. ____
2. ____
3. ____

THEMES I SAW:

1. ______________________________

2. ______________________________

3. ______________________________

Recurring thoughts (impressions, feelings, revelations) especially the ones unrelated to what I'm reading:

What did I think and feel as I read?

What Christlike attribute(s) did I notice?

REPETITIVE PHRASES THAT STUCK OUT TO ME:

1. ______________________________

2. ______________________________

3. ______________________________

How have I seen this in my life?

How can I follow the example of this person from the scriptures?

How does what I read today apply to me? Or my day today?

What does this teach me about Christ?

What am I doing well?

What questions do I have?

How did today's reading change my perspective?

What does God want me to know right now?

TODAY I AM GRATEFUL FOR:

What can I change or work on?

DATE: ____________

WHERE I READ:

____

What's happening: ______________________________

____

____

____

What doctrine is being taught? ______________________________

____

____

A talk or scripture that relates to this: ______________________________

____

____

Favorite verse from today's reading: ______________________________

____

____

INSPIRING WORDS OR VERSES:

1. ______________________________
2. ______________________________
3. ______________________________

THEMES I SAW:

1. ______________________________

2. ______________________________

3. ______________________________

Recurring thoughts (impressions, feelings, revelations) especially the ones unrelated to what I'm reading:

What did I think and feel as I read?

What Christlike attribute(s) did I notice?

REPETITIVE PHRASES THAT STUCK OUT TO ME:

1. ______________________________

2. ______________________________

3. ______________________________

→

How have I seen this in my life?

How can I follow the example of this person from the scriptures?

How does what I read today apply to me? Or my day today?

What does this teach me about Christ?

What am I doing well?

What questions do I have?

How did today's reading change my perspective?

What does God want me to know right now?

TODAY I AM GRATEFUL FOR:

What can I change or work on?

DATE: ____________

WHERE I READ:

____

What's happening: ______________________________

____

____

____

What doctrine is being taught? ______________________________

____

____

A talk or scripture that relates to this: ______________________________

____

____

Favorite verse from today's reading: ______________________________

____

____

INSPIRING WORDS OR VERSES:

1. ______________________________
2. ______________________________
3. ______________________________

THEMES I SAW:

1. ________________________________

2. ________________________________

3. ________________________________

Recurring thoughts (impressions, feelings, revelations) especially the ones unrelated to what I'm reading:

What did I think and feel as I read?

What Christlike attribute(s) did I notice?

REPETITIVE PHRASES THAT STUCK OUT TO ME:

1. ________________________________

2. ________________________________

3. ________________________________

How have I seen this in my life?

How can I follow the example of this person from the scriptures?

How does what I read today apply to me? Or my day today?

What does this teach me about Christ?

What am I doing well?

What questions do I have?

How did today's reading change my perspective?

What does God want me to know right now?

TODAY I AM GRATEFUL FOR:

What can I change or work on?

DATE: ______________

WHERE I READ:

____

What's happening: ____

____

____

____

What doctrine is being taught? ___________________________________

____

____

A talk or scripture that relates to this: ___________________________

____

____

Favorite verse from today's reading: _______________________________

____

____

INSPIRING WORDS OR VERSES:

1. ____

2. ____

3. ____

THEMES I SAW:

1. ______

2. ______

3. ______

Recurring thoughts (impressions, feelings, revelations) especially the ones unrelated to what I'm reading:

What did I think and feel as I read? ______

What Christlike attribute(s) did I notice? ______

REPETITIVE PHRASES THAT STUCK OUT TO ME:

1. ______

2. ______

3. ______

How have I seen this in my life?

How can I follow the example of this person from the scriptures?

How does what I read today apply to me? Or my day today?

What does this teach me about Christ?

What am I doing well?

What questions do I have?

How did today's reading change my perspective?

What does God want me to know right now?

TODAY I AM GRATEFUL FOR:

What can I change or work on?

DATE: ______________

WHERE I READ:

____

What's happening: ______________________________

____

____

____

What doctrine is being taught? ______________________________

____

____

A talk or scripture that relates to this: ______________________________

____

____

Favorite verse from today's reading: ______________________________

____

____

INSPIRING WORDS OR VERSES:

1. ______________________________
2. ______________________________
3. ______________________________

THEMES I SAW:

1. ______________________________

2. ______________________________

3. ______________________________

Recurring thoughts (impressions, feelings, revelations) especially the ones unrelated to what I'm reading:

What did I think and feel as I read?

What Christlike attribute(s) did I notice?

REPETITIVE PHRASES THAT STUCK OUT TO ME:

1. ______________________________

2. ______________________________

3. ______________________________

→

How have I seen this in my life?

How can I follow the example of this person from the scriptures?

How does what I read today apply to me? Or my day today?

What does this teach me about Christ?

What am I doing well?

What questions do I have?

How did today's reading change my perspective?

What does God want me to know right now?

TODAY I AM GRATEFUL FOR:

What can I change or work on?

DATE: ______________

WHERE I READ:

____

What's happening: ______________________________

____

____

____

What doctrine is being taught? ______________________________

____

____

A talk or scripture that relates to this: ______________________________

____

____

Favorite verse from today's reading: ______________________________

____

____

INSPIRING WORDS OR VERSES:

1. ______________________________
2. ______________________________
3. ______________________________

THEMES I SAW:

1. ______________________________

2. ______________________________

3. ______________________________

Recurring thoughts (impressions, feelings, revelations) especially the ones unrelated to what I'm reading:

What did I think and feel as I read? ______________________________

What Christlike attribute(s) did I notice? ______________________________

REPETITIVE PHRASES THAT STUCK OUT TO ME:

1. ______________________________

2. ______________________________

3. ______________________________

→

How have I seen this in my life?

How can I follow the example of this person from the scriptures?

How does what I read today apply to me? Or my day today?

What does this teach me about Christ?

What am I doing well?

What questions do I have?

How did today's reading change my perspective?

What does God want me to know right now?

TODAY I AM GRATEFUL FOR:

What can I change or work on?

DATE: ______________

WHERE I READ:

____

What's happening: ____

____

____

____

What doctrine is being taught? ____

____

____

A talk or scripture that relates to this: ____

____

____

Favorite verse from today's reading: ____

____

____

INSPIRING WORDS OR VERSES:

1. ____
2. ____
3. ____

THEMES I SAW:

1. ______________________________

2. ______________________________

3. ______________________________

Recurring thoughts (impressions, feelings, revelations) especially the ones unrelated to what I'm reading:

What did I think and feel as I read?

What Christlike attribute(s) did I notice?

REPETITIVE PHRASES THAT STUCK OUT TO ME:

1. ______________________________

2. ______________________________

3. ______________________________

→

How have I seen this in my life?

How can I follow the example of this person from the scriptures?

How does what I read today apply to me? Or my day today?

What does this teach me about Christ?

What am I doing well?

What questions do I have?

How did today's reading change my perspective?

What does God want me to know right now?

TODAY I AM GRATEFUL FOR:

What can I change or work on?

DATE: ____________

WHERE I READ:

____

What's happening: ______________________________

____

____

____

What doctrine is being taught? ______________________________

____

____

A talk or scripture that relates to this: ______________________________

____

____

Favorite verse from today's reading: ______________________________

____

____

INSPIRING WORDS OR VERSES:

1. ______________________________
2. ______________________________
3. ______________________________

THEMES I SAW:

1. __________
2. __________
3. __________

Recurring thoughts (impressions, feelings, revelations) especially the ones unrelated to what I'm reading:

What did I think and feel as I read?

What Christlike attribute(s) did I notice?

REPETITIVE PHRASES THAT STUCK OUT TO ME:

1.
2.
3.

→

How have I seen this in my life?

How can I follow the example of this person from the scriptures?

How does what I read today apply to me? Or my day today?

What does this teach me about Christ?

What am I doing well?

What questions do I have?

How did today's reading change my perspective?

What does God want me to know right now?

TODAY I AM GRATEFUL FOR:

What can I change or work on?

DATE: ______________

WHERE I READ:

____

What's happening: ____

____

____

____

What doctrine is being taught? _______________________________________

____

____

A talk or scripture that relates to this: _______________________________

____

____

Favorite verse from today's reading: __________________________________

____

____

INSPIRING WORDS OR VERSES:

1. ____

2. ____

3. ____

THEMES I SAW:

1. ______________________________

2. ______________________________

3. ______________________________

Recurring thoughts (impressions, feelings, revelations) especially the ones unrelated to what I'm reading:

What did I think and feel as I read? ______________________________

What Christlike attribute(s) did I notice? ______________________________

REPETITIVE PHRASES THAT STUCK OUT TO ME:

1. ______________________________

2. ______________________________

3. ______________________________

→

How have I seen this in my life?

How can I follow the example of this person from the scriptures?

How does what I read today apply to me? Or my day today?

What does this teach me about Christ?

What am I doing well?

What questions do I have?

How did today's reading change my perspective?

What does God want me to know right now?

TODAY I AM GRATEFUL FOR:

What can I change or work on?

DATE: ______________

WHERE I READ:

____

What's happening: ____

____

____

____

What doctrine is being taught? ____________________________________

____

____

A talk or scripture that relates to this: ____________________________

____

____

Favorite verse from today's reading: ______________________________

____

____

INSPIRING WORDS OR VERSES:

1. ____________________________________

2. ____________________________________

3. ____________________________________

THEMES I SAW:

1. ___

2. ___

3. ___

Recurring thoughts (impressions, feelings, revelations) especially the ones unrelated to what I'm reading:

What did I think and feel as I read?

What Christlike attribute(s) did I notice?

REPETITIVE PHRASES THAT STUCK OUT TO ME:

1. ___

2. ___

3. ___

→

How have I seen this in my life?

How can I follow the example of this person from the scriptures?

How does what I read today apply to me? Or my day today?

What does this teach me about Christ?

What am I doing well?

What questions do I have?

How did today's reading change my perspective?

What does God want me to know right now?

TODAY I AM GRATEFUL FOR:

What can I change or work on?

DATE: ______________

WHERE I READ:

____

What's happening: ____

____

____

____

What doctrine is being taught? ____

____

____

A talk or scripture that relates to this: ____

____

____

Favorite verse from today's reading: ____

____

____

INSPIRING WORDS OR VERSES:

1. ____

2. ____

3. ____

THEMES I SAW:

1. ______________________________

2. ______________________________

3. ______________________________

Recurring thoughts (impressions, feelings, revelations) especially the ones unrelated to what I'm reading:

What did I think and feel as I read? ______________________________

What Christlike attribute(s) did I notice? ______________________________

REPETITIVE PHRASES THAT STUCK OUT TO ME:

1. ______________________________

2. ______________________________

3. ______________________________

→

How have I seen this in my life?

How can I follow the example of this person from the scriptures?

How does what I read today apply to me? Or my day today?

What does this teach me about Christ?

What am I doing well?

What questions do I have?

How did today's reading change my perspective?

What does God want me to know right now?

TODAY I AM GRATEFUL FOR:

What can I change or work on?

DATE: ______________

WHERE I READ:

____

What's happening: ________________________________

____

____

____

What doctrine is being taught? ________________________________

____

____

A talk or scripture that relates to this: ________________________________

____

____

Favorite verse from today's reading: ________________________________

____

____

INSPIRING WORDS OR VERSES:

1. ________________________________
2. ________________________________
3. ________________________________

THEMES I SAW:

1. ____________________

2. ____________________

3. ____________________

Recurring thoughts (impressions, feelings, revelations) especially the ones unrelated to what I'm reading:

What did I think and feel as I read?

What Christlike attribute(s) did I notice?

REPETITIVE PHRASES THAT STUCK OUT TO ME:

1. ____________________

2. ____________________

3. ____________________

→

How have I seen this in my life?

How can I follow the example of this person from the scriptures?

How does what I read today apply to me? Or my day today?

What does this teach me about Christ?

What am I doing well?

What questions do I have?

How did today's reading change my perspective?

What does God want me to know right now?

TODAY I AM GRATEFUL FOR:

What can I change or work on?

DATE: ______________

WHERE I READ:

____

What's happening: ___________________________________

____

____

____

What doctrine is being taught? ___________________________________

____

____

A talk or scripture that relates to this: ___________________________________

____

____

Favorite verse from today's reading: ___________________________________

____

____

INSPIRING WORDS OR VERSES:

1. ___________________________________
2. ___________________________________
3. ___________________________________

THEMES I SAW:

1. ______________________________

2. ______________________________

3. ______________________________

Recurring thoughts (impressions, feelings, revelations) especially the ones unrelated to what I'm reading:

What did I think and feel as I read? ______________________________

What Christlike attribute(s) did I notice? ______________________________

REPETITIVE PHRASES THAT STUCK OUT TO ME:

1. ______________________________

2. ______________________________

3. ______________________________

→

How have I seen this in my life?

How can I follow the example of this person from the scriptures?

How does what I read today apply to me? Or my day today?

What does this teach me about Christ?

What am I doing well?

What questions do I have?

How did today's reading change my perspective?

What does God want me to know right now?

TODAY I AM GRATEFUL FOR:

What can I change or work on?

DATE: ____________

WHERE I READ:

____

What's happening: ______________________________

____

____

____

What doctrine is being taught? ______________________________

____

____

A talk or scripture that relates to this: ______________________________

____

____

Favorite verse from today's reading: ______________________________

____

____

INSPIRING WORDS OR VERSES:

1. ______________________________
2. ______________________________
3. ______________________________

THEMES I SAW:

1. ______________________________

2. ______________________________

3. ______________________________

Recurring thoughts (impressions, feelings, revelations) especially the ones unrelated to what I'm reading:

What did I think and feel as I read?

What Christlike attribute(s) did I notice?

REPETITIVE PHRASES THAT STUCK OUT TO ME:

1. ______________________________

2. ______________________________

3. ______________________________

How have I seen this in my life? ____________________

How can I follow the example of this person from the scriptures?

How does what I read today apply to me? Or my day today?

What does this teach me about Christ?

What am I doing well?

What questions do I have?

How did today's reading change my perspective?

What does God want me to know right now?

TODAY I AM GRATEFUL FOR:

What can I change or work on?

DATE: ______________

WHERE I READ:

____

What's happening: ______________________________

____

____

____

What doctrine is being taught? ______________________________

____

____

A talk or scripture that relates to this: ______________________________

____

____

Favorite verse from today's reading: ______________________________

____

____

INSPIRING WORDS OR VERSES:

1. ______________________________
2. ______________________________
3. ______________________________

THEMES I SAW:

1. ____

2. ____

3. ____

Recurring thoughts (impressions, feelings, revelations) especially the ones unrelated to what I'm reading:

What did I think and feel as I read?

What Christlike attribute(s) did I notice?

REPETITIVE PHRASES THAT STUCK OUT TO ME:

1. ____

2. ____

3. ____

How have I seen this in my life?

How can I follow the example of this person from the scriptures?

How does what I read today apply to me? Or my day today?

What does this teach me about Christ?

What am I doing well?

What questions do I have?

How did today's reading change my perspective?

What does God want me to know right now?

TODAY I AM GRATEFUL FOR:

What can I change or work on?

DATE: ______________

WHERE I READ:

____

What's happening: ____

____

____

____

What doctrine is being taught? ____

____

____

A talk or scripture that relates to this: ____

____

____

Favorite verse from today's reading: ____

____

____

INSPIRING WORDS OR VERSES:

1. ________________________________
2. ________________________________
3. ________________________________

THEMES I SAW:

1. __________

2. __________

3. __________

Recurring thoughts (impressions, feelings, revelations) especially the ones unrelated to what I'm reading:

What did I think and feel as I read?

What Christlike attribute(s) did I notice?

REPETITIVE PHRASES THAT STUCK OUT TO ME:

1.

2.

3.

→

How have I seen this in my life?

How can I follow the example of this person from the scriptures?

How does what I read today apply to me? Or my day today?

What does this teach me about Christ?

What am I doing well?

What questions do I have?

How did today's reading change my perspective?

What does God want me to know right now?

TODAY I AM GRATEFUL FOR:

What can I change or work on?

DATE: ______________

WHERE I READ:

____

What's happening: ______________________________

____

____

____

What doctrine is being taught? ______________________________

____

____

A talk or scripture that relates to this: ______________________________

____

____

Favorite verse from today's reading: ______________________________

____

____

INSPIRING WORDS OR VERSES:

1. ______________________________
2. ______________________________
3. ______________________________

THEMES I SAW:

1. ______________________________

2. ______________________________

3. ______________________________

Recurring thoughts (impressions, feelings, revelations) especially the ones unrelated to what I'm reading:

What did I think and feel as I read? ______________________________

What Christlike attribute(s) did I notice? ______________________________

REPETITIVE PHRASES THAT STUCK OUT TO ME:

1. ______________________________

2. ______________________________

3. ______________________________

→

How have I seen this in my life?

How can I follow the example of this person from the scriptures?

How does what I read today apply to me? Or my day today?

What does this teach me about Christ?

What am I doing well?

What questions do I have?

How did today's reading change my perspective?

What does God want me to know right now?

TODAY I AM GRATEFUL FOR:

What can I change or work on?

DATE: ______________

WHERE I READ:

____

What's happening: ______________________________

____

____

____

What doctrine is being taught? ______________________________

____

____

A talk or scripture that relates to this: ______________________________

____

____

Favorite verse from today's reading: ______________________________

____

____

INSPIRING WORDS OR VERSES:

1. ______________________________
2. ______________________________
3. ______________________________

THEMES I SAW:

1. ______________________________

2. ______________________________

3. ______________________________

Recurring thoughts (impressions, feelings, revelations) especially the ones unrelated to what I'm reading:

What did I think and feel as I read?

What Christlike attribute(s) did I notice?

REPETITIVE PHRASES THAT STUCK OUT TO ME:

1. ______________________________

2. ______________________________

3. ______________________________

→

How have I seen this in my life?

How can I follow the example of this person from the scriptures?

How does what I read today apply to me? Or my day today?

What does this teach me about Christ?

What am I doing well?

What questions do I have?

How did today's reading change my perspective?

What does God want me to know right now?

TODAY I AM GRATEFUL FOR:

What can I change or work on?

DATE: ____________

WHERE I READ:

____

What's happening: ______________________________

____

____

____

What doctrine is being taught? ______________________________

____

____

A talk or scripture that relates to this: ______________________________

____

____

Favorite verse from today's reading: ______________________________

____

____

INSPIRING WORDS OR VERSES:

1. ______________________________
2. ______________________________
3. ______________________________

THEMES I SAW:

1. ____________________

2. ____________________

3. ____________________

Recurring thoughts (impressions, feelings, revelations) especially the ones unrelated to what I'm reading:

What did I think and feel as I read?

What Christlike attribute(s) did I notice?

REPETITIVE PHRASES THAT STUCK OUT TO ME:

1. ____________________

2. ____________________

3. ____________________

→

How have I seen this in my life?

How can I follow the example of this person from the scriptures?

How does what I read today apply to me? Or my day today?

What does this teach me about Christ?

What am I doing well?

What questions do I have?

How did today's reading change my perspective?

What does God want me to know right now?

TODAY I AM GRATEFUL FOR:

What can I change or work on?

DATE: ____________

WHERE I READ:

____

What's happening: ______________________________

____

____

____

What doctrine is being taught? ______________________________

____

____

A talk or scripture that relates to this: ______________________________

____

____

Favorite verse from today's reading: ______________________________

____

____

INSPIRING WORDS OR VERSES:

1. ______________________________
2. ______________________________
3. ______________________________

THEMES I SAW:

1. ______________________

2. ______________________

3. ______________________

Recurring thoughts (impressions, feelings, revelations) especially the ones unrelated to what I'm reading:

____

____

____

____

____

What did I think and feel as I read? ______________________

____

____

What Christlike attribute(s) did I notice? ______________________

____

____

____

____

____

REPETITIVE PHRASES THAT STUCK OUT TO ME:

1. ______________________

2. ______________________

3. ______________________

→

How have I seen this in my life?

How can I follow the example of this person from the scriptures?

How does what I read today apply to me? Or my day today?

What does this teach me about Christ?

What am I doing well?

What questions do I have?

How did today's reading change my perspective?

What does God want me to know right now?

TODAY I AM GRATEFUL FOR:

What can I change or work on?

How have I seen this in my life?

How can I follow the example of this person from the scriptures?

How does what I read today apply to me? Or my day today?

What does this teach me about Christ?

What am I doing well?

What questions do I have?

How did today's reading change my perspective?

What does God want me to know right now?

TODAY I AM GRATEFUL FOR:

What can I change or work on?

DATE: ______________

WHERE I READ:

____

What's happening: ______________________________
____
____
____

What doctrine is being taught? ______________________________
____
____

A talk or scripture that relates to this: ______________________________
____
____

Favorite verse from today's reading: ______________________________
____
____

INSPIRING WORDS OR VERSES:

1. ______________________________
2. ______________________________
3. ______________________________

THEMES I SAW:

1. ____________________

2. ____________________

3. ____________________

Recurring thoughts (impressions, feelings, revelations) especially the ones unrelated to what I'm reading:

What did I think and feel as I read?

What Christlike attribute(s) did I notice?

REPETITIVE PHRASES THAT STUCK OUT TO ME:

1. ____________________

2. ____________________

3. ____________________

→

How have I seen this in my life?

How can I follow the example of this person from the scriptures?

How does what I read today apply to me? Or my day today?

What does this teach me about Christ?

What am I doing well?

What questions do I have?

How did today's reading change my perspective?

What does God want me to know right now?

TODAY I AM GRATEFUL FOR:

What can I change or work on?

DATE: ____________

WHERE I READ:

____

What's happening: ______________________________

____

____

____

What doctrine is being taught? ______________________________

____

____

A talk or scripture that relates to this: ______________________________

____

____

Favorite verse from today's reading: ______________________________

____

____

INSPIRING WORDS OR VERSES:

1. ______________________________
2. ______________________________
3. ______________________________

THEMES I SAW:

1. ______________________________

2. ______________________________

3. ______________________________

Recurring thoughts (impressions, feelings, revelations) especially the ones unrelated to what I'm reading:

What did I think and feel as I read? ______________________________

What Christlike attribute(s) did I notice? ______________________________

REPETITIVE PHRASES THAT STUCK OUT TO ME:

1. ______________________________

2. ______________________________

3. ______________________________

→

How have I seen this in my life?

How can I follow the example of this person from the scriptures?

How does what I read today apply to me? Or my day today?

What does this teach me about Christ?

What am I doing well?

What questions do I have?

How did today's reading change my perspective?

What does God want me to know right now?

TODAY I AM GRATEFUL FOR:

What can I change or work on?

DATE: ____________

WHERE I READ:

____

What's happening: ______________________________

____

____

____

What doctrine is being taught? ______________________________

____

____

A talk or scripture that relates to this: ______________________________

____

____

Favorite verse from today's reading: ______________________________

____

____

INSPIRING WORDS OR VERSES:

1. ______________________________
2. ______________________________
3. ______________________________

THEMES I SAW:

1. ______________________________

2. ______________________________

3. ______________________________

Recurring thoughts (impressions, feelings, revelations) especially the ones unrelated to what I'm reading:

What did I think and feel as I read?

What Christlike attribute(s) did I notice?

REPETITIVE PHRASES THAT STUCK OUT TO ME:

1. ______________________________

2. ______________________________

3. ______________________________

→

How have I seen this in my life?

How can I follow the example of this person from the scriptures?

How does what I read today apply to me? Or my day today?

What does this teach me about Christ?

What am I doing well?

What questions do I have?

How did today's reading change my perspective?

What does God want me to know right now?

TODAY I AM GRATEFUL FOR:

What can I change or work on?

DATE: ______________

WHERE I READ:

____

What's happening: ______________________________

____

____

____

What doctrine is being taught? ______________________________

____

____

A talk or scripture that relates to this: ______________________________

____

____

Favorite verse from today's reading: ______________________________

____

____

INSPIRING WORDS OR VERSES:

1. ______________________________
2. ______________________________
3. ______________________________

THEMES I SAW:

1. ______________________

2. ______________________

3. ______________________

Recurring thoughts (impressions, feelings, revelations) especially the ones unrelated to what I'm reading:

What did I think and feel as I read?

What Christlike attribute(s) did I notice?

REPETITIVE PHRASES THAT STUCK OUT TO ME:

1. ______________________

2. ______________________

3. ______________________

→

How have I seen this in my life?

How can I follow the example of this person from the scriptures?

How does what I read today apply to me? Or my day today?

What does this teach me about Christ?

What am I doing well?

What questions do I have?

How did today's reading change my perspective?

What does God want me to know right now?

TODAY I AM GRATEFUL FOR:

What can I change or work on?

DATE: ____________

WHERE I READ:

____

What's happening: ______________________________

____

____

____

What doctrine is being taught? ______________________________

____

____

A talk or scripture that relates to this: ______________________________

____

____

Favorite verse from today's reading: ______________________________

____

____

INSPIRING WORDS OR VERSES:

1. ______________________________
2. ______________________________
3. ______________________________

THEMES I SAW:

1. ______________________________

2. ______________________________

3. ______________________________

Recurring thoughts (impressions, feelings, revelations) especially the ones unrelated to what I'm reading:

What did I think and feel as I read?

What Christlike attribute(s) did I notice?

REPETITIVE PHRASES THAT STUCK OUT TO ME:

1. ______________________________

2. ______________________________

3. ______________________________

→

How have I seen this in my life? ______

How can I follow the example of this person from the scriptures?

How does what I read today apply to me? Or my day today?

What does this teach me about Christ?

What am I doing well?

What questions do I have?

How did today's reading change my perspective?

What does God want me to know right now?

TODAY I AM GRATEFUL FOR:

What can I change or work on?

DATE: ____________

WHERE I READ:

____

What's happening: ______________________________

____

____

____

What doctrine is being taught? ______________________________

____

____

A talk or scripture that relates to this: ______________________________

____

____

Favorite verse from today's reading: ______________________________

____

____

INSPIRING WORDS OR VERSES:

1. ______________________________
2. ______________________________
3. ______________________________

THEMES I SAW:

1. ________________________

2. ________________________

3. ________________________

Recurring thoughts (impressions, feelings, revelations) especially the ones unrelated to what I'm reading:

What did I think and feel as I read?

What Christlike attribute(s) did I notice?

REPETITIVE PHRASES THAT STUCK OUT TO ME:

1. ________________________

2. ________________________

3. ________________________

→

How have I seen this in my life?

How can I follow the example of this person from the scriptures?

How does what I read today apply to me? Or my day today?

What does this teach me about Christ?

What am I doing well?

What questions do I have?

How did today's reading change my perspective?

What does God want me to know right now?

TODAY I AM GRATEFUL FOR:

What can I change or work on?

NOTES

DAILY READING CHECKLIST—365 DAYS

JANUARY

					1
2	3	4	5	6	7
8	9	10	11	12	13
14	15	16	17	18	19
20	21	22	23	24	25
26	27	28	29	30	31

FEBRUARY

1	2	3	4	5	6
7	8	9	10	11	12
13	14	15	16	17	18
19	20	21	22	23	24
25	26	27	28	29	

MARCH

1					
2	3	4	5	6	7
8	9	10	11	12	13
14	15	16	17	18	19
20	21	22	23	24	25
26	27	28	29	30	31

APRIL

1	2	3	4	5	6
7	8	9	10	11	12
13	14	15	16	17	18
19	20	21	22	23	24
25	26	27	28	29	30

MAY

					1
2	3	4	5	6	7
8	9	10	11	12	13
14	15	16	17	18	19
20	21	22	23	24	25
26	27	28	29	30	31

JUNE

1	2	3	4	5	6
7	8	9	10	11	12
13	14	15	16	17	18
19	20	21	22	23	24
25	26	27	28	29	30

JULY

					1
2	3	4	5	6	7
8	9	10	11	12	13
14	15	16	17	18	19
20	21	22	23	24	25
26	27	28	29	30	31

AUGUST

					1
2	3	4	5	6	7
8	9	10	11	12	13
14	15	16	17	18	19
20	21	22	23	24	25
26	27	28	29	30	31

SEPTEMBER

1	2	3	4	5	6
7	8	9	10	11	12
13	14	15	16	17	18
19	20	21	22	23	24
25	26	27	28	29	30

OCTOBER

					1
2	3	4	5	6	7
8	9	10	11	12	13
14	15	16	17	18	19
20	21	22	23	24	25
26	27	28	29	30	31

NOVEMBER

1	2	3	4	5	6
7	8	9	10	11	12
13	14	15	16	17	18
19	20	21	22	23	24
25	26	27	28	29	30

DECEMBER

1					
2	3	4	5	6	7
8	9	10	11	12	13
14	15	16	17	18	19
20	21	22	23	24	25
26	27	28	29	30	31

ABOUT THE AUTHOR

AL CARRAWAY is a convert to the Church of Jesus Christ, writer, multi-award-winning international speaker, and author of the best-selling books *More than the Tattooed Mormon* and *Cheers to Eternity!*

Since 2010, Al has traveled Worldwide speaking about and inspiring others with her conversion and faith through difficult times. She lives with her husband, Ben, and their three kids, in Arizona, where she continues to write about her relationship with God, her experiences, lessons, and trials on www.alcarraway.com.

CFI
AN IMPRINT OF CEDAR FORT, INC.
CEDAR FORT Publishing & Media
ISBN 978-1-4621-2347-6 USA $24.99
52499
9 781462 123476